BEAUTIFULLY BROKEN

BEAUTIFULLY BROKEN

A COLLECTION OF POEMS

BRITTANY COTTEN

CONTENT WARNING

THIS BOOK CONTAINS THEMES OF SEXUAL ASSAULT, SUBSTANCE abuse, suicide, and mental health. Please be aware of these themes before reading.

PRAISE FOR BRITTANY COTTEN

"Brittany's collection of poems is a raw and honest look at personal trauma. Its visceral honesty will help any going through terrible times know they are not alone and can find their way out of their pit of despair."
   -Matthew A. Basile, Author of 'Dreaming'

"This debut poetry collection by Brittany Cotten is RAW and REAL; as you travel from piece to piece you are taken on a journey with her through the ups and downs of anxiety and depression, and I was very aware of her feelings of sadness, confusion and overwhelm. She does a beautiful job exploring the topic without judgment or embellishment."
   -Heather Melo, Author of 'Just One Night'

"Exceptionally intense, passionate poetry that will touch your soul and leave you changed. Brittany Cotten is a lady poet to look forward to!"
   -Josephine Hush, Beta Reader

"I really enjoyed how vulnerable Brittany was in writing Beautifully Broken. You can feel her pain in some of her poems. I admire how she put herself out there to not only help herself heal but to help others as well."
   -Jessica Grundy Author of 'Try Me Not'

A special thank you to the readers who have been with me every step of the way.

This poetry book is dedicated to anyone who has been in an abusive relationship, has been sexually assaulted and/or knows someone who has been. This book also goes out to EVERYONE who is dealing with their mental health, and to those who have ever lost a loved one.

To Andrew & Brandon, may no one dim your light.

A special thank you to my beta readers (Heather, Josephine, Jessica, Matthew, Adrianne, and Autumn)

Special shout out to Katherine who has been with me every step of the way in this journey! She has been such an amazing help in making this book a reality.

PLAYLIST

BELOW IS A PLAYLIST OF SONGS THAT HELPED ME IN MY PAST AND some that have helped me to this day, when I get overwhelmed or triggered. I hope one, some or all these songs help you as they have helped me at one point or another.

1. Stronger - Mandisa
2. Beautifully Broken - Plumb
3. Jesus, Take the Wheel - Carrie Underwood
4. Warrior - Demi Lovato
5. Prize Worth Fighting For - Jamie Kimmett
6. White Crown - Grayson Webb
7. Drive - Incubus
8. More Hearts than Mine - Ingrid Andress
9. Leave Me A Memory - Fillmore
10. Die from a Broken Heart - Maddie & Tae
11. Heather Gray - Grayson Webb
12. Down - Jamie Kimmett
13. Burdens - Jamie Kimmett
14. Even Then - Micah Tyler
15. Canyon - Ellie Holcomb

CONTENTS

CHAPTER 1
BEAUTIFULLY BROKEN

I'M BROKEN
I'm bruised
I didn't have much to lose
Until you took me by the hand
And gave me the world
Just to tear it apart
I'm broken, I'm bruised
I've got nothing to lose?
I lost myself, trying to please everyone else.
Now I know the truth.
Broken
Bruised
Nothing to lose
So I'll hold onto the truth
You weren't good for me
You broke me down
You bruised my crown
And now I know, I am better off without you
I can be broken, I can be bruised

But I have so much more to lose
I AM broken, I AM bruised
I AM Beautiful.
Beautifully broken

CHAPTER 2
I GOT!

I got pain, flowing through my veins
  All because you went insane.
  I got my heart ripped, limb from limb
  All because I took one look at him.
  I got my mind in a knot
  All because you didn't stop.
  I got my mind on how to get free
  Because, I don't want you next to me.
  I got scars and bruises
  Asking why I'm being so foolish.
  I got my head between my knees, begging you, please
  Don't do this to me.
  You said you were sorry, that you would stop
  But look around, I'm still in shock.
  I got my mouth shut
  Because you told me not to say much.
  I got my shoes on, ready to run
  But you pulled me back, and we all heard that thud
  Echoing down the hall.

I got a headache
All because you didn't want a heartache.
I got something
I don't want
I Got!

CHAPTER 3
THREE YEARS AGO

THREE YEARS AGO,
     if you were to tell me
     Where I would be today
     I'd laugh, and say "No way".
     If you knew me back then,
     you would say the same.
     I still can't believe how much I've changed.
     I've loved.
     I've lost.
     But I'll never be the same.
     I felt like giving up, throwing in the towel
     Then you came and saved me.
     I'm finally happy, finally free.
     Three years ago, I was miserable
     Burning bridges Left, and Right
     With no end in sight
     No family, No friends
     Just me and my thoughts.
     Three years ago.

CHAPTER 4
LOVING FATHER

I HEAR RAIN DROPS
  DRIP,DRIP,DRIP
  I see people walk in and out of my life
  Goodbye one says,
  Hello says another
  I miss you my loving father
  As I lay to rest at night,
  "Everything will be fine!"
  A whisper comes from behind.

DEDICATED TO MY FATHER MICHAEL COTTEN, MAY HE REST IN paradise.

GONE BUT NEVER FORGOTTEN.
  09/11/2009

CHAPTER 5
NOTHING ON YOU!

You laugh, as I cry.
   You tell me all these beautiful lies.
   It's hard to believe
   I couldn't see
   You were nothing but a cheat
   You broke me in two
   Oh how that couldn't do
   I laugh, as I look back
   You broke me down
   Wouldn't let me be me
   You hurt me more than once
   And I was to blame?
   Did nothing right,
   but I held on tight
   to all the good times, even through our fights
   It hurt me more to stay
   then it did to walk away
   I just wanted peace, to be happy
   yet, you were a demon in disguise

'Misery wants company'
has nothing on you!

CHAPTER 6
I CAN SEE

I can see the lies
through your eyes.
I can see the pain
you hide inside.
I can see you unhappy
With or without me.
I can see everything.
You say that you love me.
You say that you care.
But, you don't hear the pain
in the words that you share.
I can see it's killing you inside
So just speak your mind
Just tell me
Just say it
Just let it all out
You're not in love with me
Like you were before her.

CHAPTER 7
COLOR MY DAY

IF I WERE TO COLOR MY DAY
    It'd be a stormy gray.
    I have nothing more to say
    He tells me to let it all out
    Then he starts to shout
    So why even try?
    I keep it all inside
    All to myself.
    Stormy Gray
    Doesn't get enough credit
    I say
    It's nothing to be shy about
    Color my day
    A stormy gray
    Just get out of my way
    I can't take this pain
    Color MY day

CHAPTER 8
ROOM 113

Room 113
  Away from you
  It's so cold!
  Wanting you near
  Room 113
  What does this even mean?
  Can't get you out of my mind.
  I'm still in a twine
  Wishing I could rewind
  Room 113
  Come back to me
  Got a lot to work on?
  I want to work it out with you.
  Please don't go
  Please don't leave
  Please come back for me
  Room 113
  This is crazy!
  four grown men,

Gathered in the room
Hot breath filling the air,
Gum chewing, in my ear
and all I can think about is you.
Room 113

CHAPTER 9
EMOTIONS

ANGER

No matter where I turn,
You're always there.
I can't get away from you no matter what
I say or do.
I can't run from you or the pain you cause.

DEPRESSION

Oh how I wish I never saw you.
You keep me grounded,
kept chained to the bed.
Everywhere I go,
you're always there to comfort my anger.

HAPPINESS

Happiness? What are you?
I hardly see you
I have searched a thousand miles

With you nowhere in sight.
I could never win, when it comes to fighting for you.

STUPIDITY
    I can't help the laugh
    that escapes my lips.
    Why is it that, you follow me everywhere
    And fog up my common sense?

CHAPTER 10
HE'S NO YOU

You don't make me happy.
You don't make me proud.
You don't make me smile.
I just want to be happy!
I just want to be proud!
I just want to smile!
He makes me happy.
He makes me proud.
He makes me smile.
He's no you.
I can laugh with him.
I can cry with him.
I can talk with him.
I can be myself
And no one else!
I'm finally happy
I'm finally free
No red flags, blinding me
When I laugh, he smiles
Like it's music to his ears

When I cry, he holds me tight
Tells me everything will be alright
When I talk, he looks me in the eyes
Like it's the most important thing in his life.
I am damaged and broken
A broken puzzle piece and he is the glue
I'm so much better without you
He's no you!

CHAPTER 11
BLOOD

Just because you're blood
Doesn't mean I love you more
Doesn't make it hurt any less
Just because you're blood
Doesn't make it right
Just because you're blood
Doesn't mean I'll drop everything
Without a fight
Just because you're blood
Doesn't mean you're 'family'
I'll say this..
I love you, I always will
But sometimes it's not enough.
I love you, but I'll love you from afar.
Just
Because
You're.
Blood

CHAPTER 12
AFRAID TO CLOSE

Afraid.
Afraid to close my eyes at night
Afraid of what I'll see
Reliving every bad scene, on rewind
Afraid to close my eyes
Afraid I'd see him
See him hold me down,
forcing himself inside of me
See him holding my mouth shut, as I try to scream.
Scream for him to let me go
To let me free
Scream for him to get off me,
Scream for someone, anyone to help me
and watch as no one comes.
Afraid to close my eyes
Afraid to hear his voice, against my ear
Afraid to close my eyes
Afraid no one will be there
Be there for me

Be there
to get him off
to make him stop
Afraid to close my eyes
Afraid he will kill me in my dreams.

CHAPTER 13
ALL OUT OF PLACE

All out of place
That's no mistake
I feel like an unfinished puzzle piece
So pick up my pieces
And put me back together
All out of place
Where shall I go?
What shall I do?
So come to me
And you can be the best thing for me
All out of place
With no one to chase my fears away
No one to hold
No one to love
No one to turn to, except my rug
All out of place
There's things to change
But take your time
This isn't a race

Because
I'm all out of place

CHAPTER 14
PAIN AIN'T A GAME

Its funny how
you think my pain
is just a game
But in reality
all you want
is to be me
Haters will always
be haters
Just like players
will always be players
If my pain is just
a game
let me go first
Haha.
Look who's
laughing now
Now you're not
ever
getting a shot to break my heart

Checkmate
I win
Ain't ever letting you in again.

CHAPTER 15
I DON'T WANT IT

I don't want it.
I don't want the nightmare
Don't want the lies I hear
Don't want drama.
I don't want it.
I don't want to fight for happiness
I don't want to fight for the fun of it
I don't want it.
I don't want the anger or the depression
I don't want it.
I don't want the disappointment
Or the fakes or hypocrites
I don't want to sit and wait for things to get right.
I don't want it.
I don't want these tears or the fears
that come along with all these memories
I don't want it.

CHAPTER 16
ALONE & AFRAID

I'M ALL ALONE AND AFRAID
  by the words that you say
  It's a prison for me
  I'm alone and afraid
  Searching for the words to say
  I'm stuck with the decisions
  that I've made
  Alone
  Afraid
  Why did I choose to stay?
  You kept me on my toes.
  In a room full of people, I feel all alone.
  Afraid of the unknown
  I couldn't keep my hands to myself
  and now all I want to do is run
  Yet, my feet stay planted and I can't look away
  Alone
  Afraid
  Alone & afraid.

CHAPTER 17
TRAVEL

When you've traveled the world
searching for the seven seas,
Will you finally be happy?
When you've traveled the world
With your best friend
And you've seen all
There is to see
Will you still
Want to be next to me?
When you've traveled the world
Leaving me behind
Am I on your mind,
As much as you're on mine?
You went and traveled the world,
Without me
And let me just say
That was the best thing for me
For you
For us.

Go on and live your life to the fullest.
Travel long and far
Go on and live your life
Travel.

CHAPTER 18
"DEAR GOD"

I REMEMBER THAT NIGHT
like the back of my hand
Hitch hiking at dawn
As I yawn
He stopped in front of me
Picked me up
Took me to his place
TV in the background
As I chugged down the drink
Next thing I knew, he was standing next to me
As I made my way up the stairs
Stumbling and grasping onto the wall
He held my waist
As he threw me on to the bed, with a bounce
The room wouldn't stop spinning
He had a gun to my head
I was terrified and closed my eyes
As the tears pushed through
Running down my cheeks
I cried, and I cried. This just isn't right.

I whispered in to the dark room "Dear god, please
help me"
Just as I heard his pants hit the floor
And he snatched what didn't belong to him
One friend, two friends, three friends and him…
I was used and abused
Until I ended up on the street
I still can't believe
A week was taken away from me

CHAPTER 19
MEMORY!

I REMEMBER
that day, we were playing out late
I remember
dad saying "time to come in"
you rolled your eyes to the back of your head
I remember
running to his arms
as he made his way back in
I remember
all the teasing
for being daddy's little girl
I remember
It all
The cook outs
The parties
The Sunday feasts
I remember
The good times,
before the clouds came over our heads

and tore it all away.
Memories are all I hold onto,
as days turn into years.

CHAPTER 20
DEAR POEM

Dear Drugs and alcohol
I would like to tell you
You fog up my common sense and enable it
You tell me
You can make me feel oh so good
You tell me
Its okay to sit back, relax and drink it all away
The pain, and the misery.
You tell me
No one loves me,
so it's okay to get lost at the bottom of the bottle.
I would like to tell you no more.
I am stronger than before.
So during our next encounter
I just might break your needle
And throw the bottle against the wall
And watch as the liquid drips down slowly
You always made me feel a certain kind of way
Until I didn't have a word to say
I always leaned your way

when I wanted it all to go away.
It started off because a man took me off the street.
Ended with me needing to block out that memory.
No more! I can be happy without your 'help'

Yours truly,
   A girl with mystery

CHAPTER 21
CRAZY!

If I could express how you make me feel
They might lock me up
and
throw away the key.
I might sounds crazy
but you're the one for me
The way you look at me
makes me wanna scream
The way you smile
makes me go crazy
Never felt this way before
just wanna run down the street
screaming your name
Oh how your name makes me
Tingle from my head to my feet
How your laugh makes
my knees go weak
How you show me love,
like no other before you.
Being with you makes me melt,

breaking into a million pieces
because I know you will be there,
to put me back together again.
I might be crazy
but you're the one for me.

CHAPTER 22
IN THE AIR FORCE!

You're in the Air Force
  In the Air Force away from me
  In the Air Force yippee
  In the Air Force leaving me
  In the Air Force with no more pain
  In the Air Force how I wish that could be me
  In the Air Force yippee
  You're in the Air Force
  In the Air Force what about me?
  In the Air Force good luck on your knees.
  In the Air Force hope to see you soon
  In the Air Force I don't wanna lose you
  In the Air Force fighting over there
  while I'm here, fighting not to shed a tear
  In the Air Force making dad so proud
  In the Air Force yippee
  You're in the Air Force
  In the Air Force oh so sorry
  In the Air Force oh so frightening

In the Air Force oh how I miss you
In the Air Force I'm oh so proud
Goodbye for now!
I'll see you when you make it home again.

CHAPTER 23
SILENCED

I'm always silenced
when I try to let the world know
I'm slowly dying inside
I'm always silenced
When I try to tell my truth
When I don't feel like growing old,
In a world so cold
I'm always silenced
When I say what I've been through
Always silenced
When I make you feel a certain kind of way
I'm crying inside
I'm dying inside
The world never understood the girls like me
So strong
So brave
Pushing through what was supposed to break her.
Can't you see?
This is just as hard for me!
I'm trying to heal,

But all I feel
Is you trying to silence me

Don't silence girl's like me
    we won't stand down
    we'll just stand tall, together.

CHAPTER 24
SUICIDE

Suicide
It's always on my mind.
Wanting it all to end, in one night.
Would anyone really care?
Would anyone shed a tear?
Suicide.
I look at the pills
I look at the bourbon
in my hands.
Suicide
It's on my mind
It's like a broken record,
Begging me to do it on repeat.
Take those pills!
Use that rope!
Pick up that Knief
and slit your throat!
Suicide
Always on my mind.
It won't stop

Reminding me I have no family, I have no friends.
No one to miss me
No one to care.
The night mares will end
The shakes will stop.

SUICIDE

DEAR READERS - AN AUTHORS NOTE

Dear readers,

This book was made during a hard time in my life. You see, writing poetry was my escape from such a hard reality. This is just a few, of many poems that I grew up rereading over and over again, as I dealt with all the ups and downs. As well as dealing with my mental health.

In no way is this giving it an 'okay' to do such things like drugs, alcohol, or trying to end your life. You are loved and wanted. So don't even try it, your story isn't over yet!

I used reading as another escape from reality and I hope this book can bring an escape for someone as well as letting them know they are not alone.

On the next page will be numbers and websites for anyone needing someone to talk to.

Always remember you are never alone.

I know it may be hard to reach out, but just know you are strong, brave and worth so much more.

Never let anyone dim your light, or mess up your crown.

. . .

Love always,
Brittany Cotten
XXX

Love always,
Brittany Cotten
XXX

AUTHORS NOTE CONTINUED - A NOTE ON EACH POEM

I wrote 'Beautifully Broken' because; I have healed and have come so far in my life.

Don't get me wrong, I still have moments when I don't feel good enough or like I am too broken for a future worth living for. So I sat down and wrote to myself, and then I turned my letter into a poem. I have so much to lose if I were to give it all away. I may be broken or my ego may be bruised, but I am worth all the love and respect I see others have.

I wrote 'I got', during a time when I was in a toxic relationship. So many friends and family warned me about how toxic this relationship was, and I didn't listen. I made my choice and even though it wasn't healthy for me I didn't care at the time. So many say "Just leave" but I never did, I couldn't understand why and I couldn't explain it but I never did. So 'I Got!' Was born. I got a relationship that I didn't want yet, I didn't leave, I wasn't strong enough. I am here to tell anyone dealing with it, I know how it feels to be told to just leave, and I also know how it feels to not want to leave, to believe that he can change. I know it is easier said than done, but you're so much stronger than this. You are not alone. You deserve so much better!

I wrote '3 years ago' during a time I was beginning to heal. I was told that if I continued down the path that I was going then I would end up in jail or dead. I laughed and said "Okay, if its my time, it's my time" I was suicidal, an alcoholic, smoking, a runaway every chance I got, etc. Everyone knew I was going nowhere fast. So once I gave my life back to the Lord, I became happy, Suicide was the last thing on my mind, and I turned a full 360 in my life. I was proud. So during that time I was like no one would believe that I became a better person.

I wrote 'loving father', the day after I was informed my father passed away after being in a medically induced coma. I was honestly heartbroken. He was a great father, even though behind closed doors, there were questionable moments. I made this poem and was going to read it at his funeral, but I couldn't stop crying. It means so much to me. "GOODBYE ONE SAYS. HELLO SAYS ANOTHER" was toward my father passing and my aunt being pregnant with my cousin. It also meant so many abandon me, but so many come into my life at the same time.

I wrote 'Nothing on you' , and it was because an ex was toxic, he was manipulative and always cheating on me. He even dated my so-called best friend while we were dating and everyone in school told me his current knott in his belt.

He gaslit me every chance he got and would blame everything he did on me. I was always told to ignore it, leave him, blah blah misery wants company, but honestly, that was nothing compared to him.

I WROTE ' I CAN SEE', BECAUSE I WAS IN A RELATIONSHIP WITH a man who claimed he loved me, but after a while, they became just words. I later found out he was talking to another girl. So it not only hurt me,but put me into the mind space that I would never be good enough, so I continued to put it into other relationships. Constantly asking someone, "What's on your mind?" "Let it all out, I won't judge" and so on, and so on.

I WROTE 'COLOR MY DAY', I WROTE IT DURING A DARK TIME. I always compared my days to colors, and That day was a stormy gray because I was numb.

I WROTE 'ROOM 113' WHEN I WAS GETTING TREATMENT FOR my PTSD. I was in a hotel room as I was waiting for my boyfriend to come back and I started to get in my feelings, and then I started having flashbacks of when I was taken and this time the flashbacks felt real. It felt like they were in the hotel room with me. So I wrote a letter to myself that It wasn't real, no matter how real it felt, it wasn't real. That the hot breath I felt hit my neck, sending goosebumps down my arms was not real. That the laughing, and disgusting talking that they were doing, was not real. I later flipped it into the poem 'room 113' to show even though I was in the middle of a breakdown, my boyfriend was my safe place, and he helped me through the episode, even though he was not there.

. . .

I wrote 'Emotions', to show that it is okay to feel all these emotions, but what wasn't okay was how I was dealing with them. The choices I was making weren't okay. So I wrote to them to let them know I knew they were there but I wasn't going to let that affect me.

I wrote ' He's no you' , towards staff members in the all girls school I was in , in prescott,AZ

I get asked "Is this guy real?" No. At least not yet (HAHA) It was more numerous staff, than just one person. They helped me realize I am strong, brave and worth it.

I wrote 'Blood' , during a time when some of my own blood became toxic for me, so I decided to give space, so I could grow.

I wrote 'Afraid to close' , because there was a time where I was so afraid to sleep, afraid he would find me and kill me. So this one means a lot to me, even though it's so real and scary. I wanted to put this one in the book because I blamed everyone but the one who needed the blame, which was the man that took me against my will.

I wrote 'All out of place' , because I have always felt like my life was a mess, that I was a broken puzzle missing pieces and I just wanted to find someone or anyone that would be strong enough to stand by me during my episodes and help me put my life back together. I just wanted someone there, but soon I realized the only one I really needed, I always had. The lord never left my side. Not even for a minute.

I WROTE ' PAIN AIN'T A GAME', BECAUSE I WAS WITH SOMEONE who thought it was the funniest thing to see me in pain, so he would put me down, cheat, lie, gaslight me, etc. So I told myself enough is enough. So if he thought playing with my heart was a game, I was going to beat him at his own game.

I WROTE 'I DON'T WANT IT', BECAUSE I WAS DONE. I WAS READY to end it all. The nightmares, the flashbacks, the paranoia. I was just done, I didn't want the pain or the memories. I wanted to end my life so I didn't have to deal with all of this.

I WROTE 'ALONE & AFRAID', BECAUSE I FELT ALONE AND I WAS afraid of what the future held. Like as a child I was molested, I was kidnapped, raped and beat so I was constantly in fear that history would repeat itself.

I WROTE 'TRAVEL', BECAUSE ANYONE I LOVED OR CARED ABOUT would always leave. So travel was more of a phrase than it was actually traveling.

I WROTE 'DEAR GOD', BECAUSE THAT IS WHAT HAPPENED. I turned away from god and began running away. So when I was in that room I prayed and cried, and prayed again and again, and I even turned and said "Why me?" I then shut off any contact with him because I felt like he didn't care, that no one did, so I turned off any and every emotion for a while.

I wrote 'memory', because my life was good, until it wasn't so I wanted to hold on to the good memories when my family was a family.

I wrote 'Dear Poem', when I was 17 and in rehab. To say I was a drug addict wouldn't be the full truth per say... I would abuse prescribed meds, mine or my friends, or my friends parents pills to the point it would numb me, I could forget everything. I'm not proud of that, but I am proud that I made it out of what was to break me. I am blessed I didn't OD. I still struggle with alcohol, just like the rest, but I refuse to take any medicine that is strong like that. I take the basic ones for migraines or cramps but other than that, I refuse to fill them if they are prescribed.

I wrote 'crazy', because I was and am in a relationship where I think 'HE IS THE ONE'

I felt like I was one of those crazy chicks off of 'LIFETIME' because I have never felt this way before. I mean I would never do anything like a lifetime movie does, but I definitely question myself. Is this really love? Or are you grasping onto the fact that he hasn't left, or he is your safe spot?

I wrote 'In the Air Force', because my older brother and I were super close but he left as soon as he turned 18 to the Air force so I haven't talked to him much in years. It breaks my heart that my brother, the best friend of best friends, who did everything together left to fight for our freedom and all I could do is worry until I heard something from my family about his whereabouts. So I made a poem, dedicated to him. To let him know that I love and care about him and I am so proud of him!

I wrote 'Silenced', because I honestly feel like so many women, girls, boys and even men who are survivors (Warriors) are silenced when they try to speak up and I feel like that isn't right whatsoever. So if they don't have a voice, or their voice was taken from them, then I would be their voice!

I wrote 'Suicide', during the time I was suicidal because its true. You're in constant battle with yourself like "End it, don't end it" and sometimes your body wins, and you end it and sometimes your mind wins and you don't. This poem was made to show that no matter how much the demon is whispering in your ear, that you would be better off dead. That's not true! You are worth so much more and God wants you to know your story isn't over!

VALUABLE RESOURCES

Your mental health is important! You are important! If you are in mental crisis, please seek help using these free resources, available night and day.

Suicide and crisis hotline:
    Open 24 hours a day
    Languages: English and Spanish
    Call: 988
    National Suicide Prevention Lifeline
    Open 24 hours a day
    Languages: English and Spanish
    800 - 273 - TALK (8255)
    DoD safe helpline (Sexual Assault survivor)
    Chat: Online.SafeHelpline.Org
    Call: 877- 995 - 5247
    Discuss: SafeHelpRoom.Org
    Veterans Crisis Hotline
    Open 24 hours a day

Confidential
For Veterans and their families
Call: 988 and press '1'
Text: 838255

You are not alone.

ABOUT BRITTANY

Brittany Cotten lives in a small town in Oklahoma with her two children, her four god-children, her boyfriend, best friend, and a dog named Zeus.

You will always catch her working, spending time with her family or with her nose in a book.

She has loved writing since she was eight years old. Brittany used to rewrite her favorite TV shows to have a better ending or favorite movie to make sure she was included in the story.

Iff you don't find Brittany nose deep in a book, you will find her trying to change the world, one word at a time.

www.ingramcontent.com/pod-product-compliance
Lightning Source LLC
Chambersburg PA
CBHW050612160726
48003CB00003B/1152